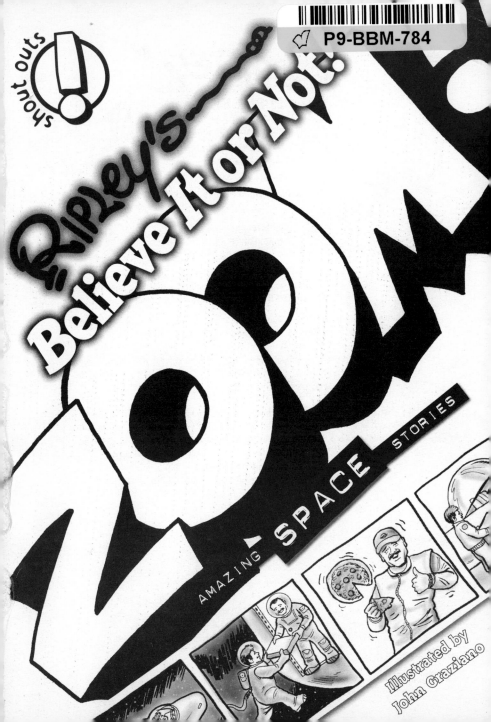

shout outs

P9-BBM-784

Ripley's
Believe It or Not!

ZOOM

AMAZING SPACE STORIES

Illustrated by
John Graziano

PUBLISHING

Publishing Director Anne Marshall
Editorial Director Becky Miles
Art Director Sam South
Senior Designer Michelle Foster
Assistant Editor Charlotte Howell
Design Ark Creative
Reprographics Juice Creative
Consultant Chris Oxlade

Published by Scholastic Inc. SCHOLASTIC and associated logos are trademarks and/or
registered trademarks of Scholastic Inc., 557 Broadway, New York , NY 10012

ISBN 978-0-545-38076-8

12 11 10 9 8 7 6 5 4 3 2 1   11 12 13 14 15 16/0

Printed in the U.S.A.   40
First printing, September 2011

PUBLISHER'S NOTE
While every effort has been made to verify the accuracy of the entries in this book,
the Publisher cannot be held responsible for any errors contained in the work.
They would be glad to receive any information from readers.

WARNING
Some of the stunts and activities in this book are undertaken by experts and should
not be attempted by anyone without adequate training and supervision.

INTRODUCING...
JOHN GRAZIANO

John, Ripley's very own cartoonist, has drawn every cartoon in this wacky book of space stories and facts.

A new Ripley's cartoon has been produced every day for the past 90 years by a dedicated Ripley's cartoonist. John is only the eighth person to take on this role. Amazingly, he got himself the job 25 years after sending his drawings to Ripley's as a teenager!

SPEEDY QUESTIONS!

1. Q: What tools do you use for your drawings?
A: My actual drawings are done the old-fashioned way: with pencil, pen and ink, brush and ink to paper. For airbrushing and coloring, I use a Wacom digital tablet.

2. Q: If you hadn't become an artist what would you be?
A: I actually wanted to be a paleontologist and dig up fossils! I do that as a hobby though.

3. Q: What is your favorite space story in this book?
A: I liked the one about the "Star Wars-themed" wedding.

4. Q: What do you think aliens look like?
A: Different to Earth people!

HOW TO DRAW A...
ROCKET

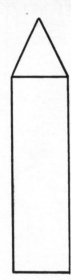

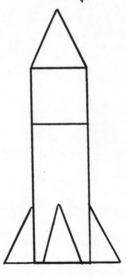

2. About one-third from the top of the rectangle, draw a line. Add three triangles to the bottom of the rectangle.

3. Divide up the top section of the rectangle like this.

1. Draw a triangle on top of a long, tall rectangle, like this.

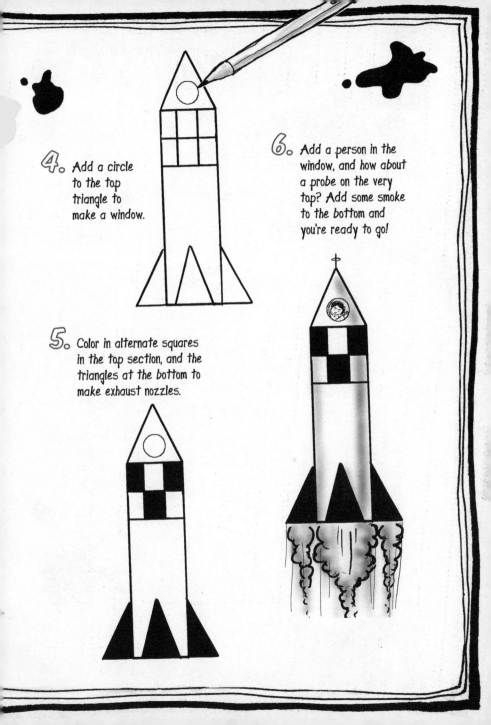

4. Add a circle to the top triangle to make a window.

6. Add a person in the window, and how about a probe on the very top? Add some smoke to the bottom and you're ready to go!

5. Color in alternate squares in the top section, and the triangles at the bottom to make exhaust nozzles.

ZOOM!

space

You won't believe the wacky stories you're about to read when you dip inside this fun-packed book! Meet Ham the space-traveling chimp, a man who built a UFO landing port in his backyard, the tortoises that flew around the Moon, and many more!
It's Ripley's Shout Outs!

THE UNIVERSE...

Upsizing
The Universe is expanding every single second.

The Universe is a busy place. There are galaxies, planets, moons, stars, gas, dust, black holes, dark energy, comets, asteroids, and the odd satellite and spacecraft zipping about. But it's not crowded out there; there's not a traffic jam in sight. The Universe is so big that even if you traveled in a spaceship forever, you would never reach its edge.

Center point?
The Universe has no center.

Gigantic galaxies
There may be as many as 100 billion galaxies in the Universe. Our very own galaxy, the Milky Way, is not the biggest, but it is still ginormous. It contains roughly 200 billion stars!

THERE'S NOTHING BIGGER!

Seeing the light
For hundreds of thousands of years after it formed, the Universe was a really dark place, because no stars had started shining. Look at it now!

It's a shore thing
The Universe contains more stars than Earth has grains of sand.

Wotta lotta space
The Universe is a mind-bogglingly big space, but actually has hardly anything in it. Think of it this way—it's like having a building 20 miles long, 20 miles wide, and 20 miles high that contains just one grain of sand.

Just a *bit* old
As late as 1820, the Universe was thought to be 6,000 years old. It is now believed to be between 15 and 20 billion years old— that's 15 billion years or over a hundred million times older than the oldest person!

SOLAR SYSTEM

Who's the fastest person in the world? Olympic gold medalist Usain Bolt? Wrong. We're the fastest! We all zip around the Sun on our planet at more than 62,000 mph. We're joined by seven other planets, also making a never-ending sprint around the Sun—each one in its own time and place, making up the Solar System.

JUPITER

MARS

In for the ride
All the planets are heading in the same direction around the Sun—counter-clockwise.

EARTH

You are here!

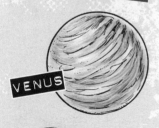

VENUS

MERCURY

Tiny us
The Sun makes up 99.86 percent of the Solar System's mass! And 73 percent of the Sun is hydrogen, so most matter in the Solar System is hydrogen. If you collected all the planets and asteroids together, they'd make up a minute part of the Solar System's mass—only 0.14 percent. That's tiny!

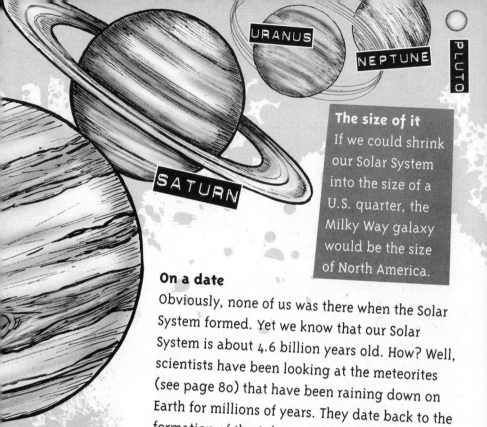

URANUS

NEPTUNE

PLUTO

SATURN

The size of it
If we could shrink our Solar System into the size of a U.S. quarter, the Milky Way galaxy would be the size of North America.

On a date
Obviously, none of us was there when the Solar System formed. Yet we know that our Solar System is about 4.6 billion years old. How? Well, scientists have been looking at the meteorites (see page 80) that have been raining down on Earth for millions of years. They date back to the formation of the Solar System and, yes, you've guessed it—they're all 4.6 billion years old.

Think again
There are eight planets in our Solar System, not nine as was previously thought. Pluto has been downgraded to a dwarf planet. This is an object orbiting the Sun that is a sphere, but that astronomers think is too small to be a proper planet.

Get in line
Want to remember the order of the planets from the Sun? Say this to yourself—*My Very Energetic Mommy Just Served Us Noodles*. The initial letter of each word is the starting letter of the planets in turn.

THE SUN

Is the Sun a warming friend that makes pretty colors at dawn and dusk? Or is it an immense, monstrous super-power of burning gas, a speck of which would kill you in a flash from 99 miles away?

THE SURFACE

93 MILLION MILES

Scary star

The Sun is a star, 333,000 times the mass of Earth, with an internal pressure so enormous that nuclear reactions take place all the time, like billions of nuclear weapons going off every second.

THE SUN IS 93 MILLION MILES

Out like a light

If the Sun stopped shining, no one on Earth would know for 8 minutes because that's how long it takes for sunlight to travel from the Sun to Earth.

On the bright side

Night owls must get confused in Spitsbergen, Norway, where, for 3½ months every year, the Sun shines continuously—both day and night.

OF THE SUN IS 9,930° F

FROM EARTH

Singing Sun
The Sun actually sings to itself! Its surface wobbles in and out, which would make a rumbling sound—if we could hear it!

Old flame
The Sun is about one-third as old as the Universe, and is about halfway through its life. Middle-aged, eh? Still looking good!

Greedy!
The Sun burns up some 20 billion million tons of hydrogen in a year. That's a lot of fuel!

Cold comfort
Without the Sun, Earth's temperature would be about -454°F. With no light or heat, nothing would live here at all.

Afraid of the dark
When the Moon positions itself between the Sun and Earth, it blocks out the light. That moment is called a solar eclipse, and to witness one is a spooky sensation. No solar eclipse can last longer than 7 minutes 58 seconds because of the speed at which the Moon moves.

GROUND CONTROL

It can be tricky using a **toolbox** in space—your screwdriver floats away! To help with ordinary maintenance, astronauts use Velcro belts to keep their **tools** at hand, and hook their feet under straps or bars to stop themselves from drifting *around*.

In a whirl

With its rings spinning around it, Saturn is like
one giant hula-hooper! If you could get closer, you
would see that the rings are made up of billions of
snowballs, some as small as a fingernail,
some bigger than a house!

Only one spacecraft has ever visited Uranus. In
1986, Voyager 2 flew past the planet and took
thousands of photos. Voyager 2 then carried on to
Neptune, and beyond. In fact, it's still exploring the
farthest parts of the Solar System today.

Everyone say cheese

Tony Rafaat from Alberta, Canada, made his
own weather balloon with a camera attached.
His balloon reached an incredible

117,595 FEET

and traveled 62 miles before it landed and Tony
was able to retrieve it and reveal the stunning
pictures it had taken on its journey.

Ripley's
SPACECHIMP

One of the first Americans in space was Ham the chimp! He was trained to perform tasks in his space capsule.

Wearing a specially designed spacesuit, Ham was launched into space in 1961.

He traveled at speeds of 5,000 mph for 16 minutes 39 seconds, before splashing back down to Earth.

On his return, he was rewarded with an apple and half an orange to celebrate his successful mission!

ALIENS!

Hearing you loud and clear

In 1967, a weird ticking radio signal from space was detected. Scientists set about trying to explain it and excitedly called the project "LGM" for "Little Green Men." The sound turned out to be a type of spinning star called a pulsar—sadly, no aliens were found!

AMAZING!

Time traveler

The *Voyager 1* space probe was launched by NASA in 1977. Scientists think it should finally reach some stars after traveling for more than 80,000 years. Plenty of time to bump into other beings along the way!

They're here!

A 2010 April Fool's report in a newspaper almost led to a whole town being evacuated. Its front-page article described a UFO landing near Jafr in Jordan. Residents panicked, keeping their children home from school. Jafr's mayor was fooled by the prank and sent security forces in search of the aliens. He was on the point of emptying the town of its 13,000 residents when alarmed newspaper journalists came clean.

AWESOME!

Cosmic cuisine

Joe Simonton said that he met aliens in 1961 and they gave him several salt-free pancakes. It was an interesting choice of visiting gift from people who might have picked up anything from the whole Universe! Joe was from then on nicknamed "Pancake Joe."

Close encounters?

In March 2011, NASA scientist Richard Hoover announced that he'd found signs of life from outer space! At last! He said he found alien bacteria (living things that can only be seen under a microscope) inside a meteorite that had landed on Earth. Some people thought, though, that because the meteorite had been on Earth for a hundred years, it was pretty hard to say whether the bacteria were "foreign." That's disappointing.

Wave of doubt

Loads of people saw a strange vessel flying over a church in Papua New Guinea, in June 1959. Father Gill and his congregation saw "a circular vessel with rails, like the bridge of a boat." The crew of four was leaning over the rails and when the people on the ground waved at them, they waved back!

WOW!

Ripley's

WEIGHTLESS WHISKERS

When male astronauts first shaved in space, their weightless whiskers floated up to the ceiling. So NASA developed a special razor that sucked in the whiskers like a vacuum cleaner.

BEFORE

AFTER

Over ten years, the Mir space station threw over 200 garbage bags into space. They are all still orbiting Earth.

SOMETHING TO WAG ABOUT

A comet called Hyakutake had a tail 360 million miles long—nearly four times longer than the distance from Earth to the Sun! In 1996, it passed closer to Earth than any other comet in about 200 years.

WHOOOSH

It was discovered in January 1996 by Yuji Hyakutake, from southern Japan, who found it by looking only through a pair of binoculars! By March, it was visible with the naked eye, traveling fast in the sky. It won't return to our Solar System for another 70,000 years!

WE HAVE LIFT OFF!

A house in Chattanooga, Tennessee, that's shaped like a flying saucer was sold at an auction in 2008 for a down-to-earth price of $135,000. Built in 1970, shortly after the first Moon landing, it has small, square windows and is perched on six "landing gear" legs. It also has a retractable staircase at the entrance for either humans or aliens.

Me and my shadow

A solar eclipse occurs when the Moon moves between Earth and the Sun. Not only does the day turn black, but temperatures suddenly drop, birds fly to roost, and an

EERIE WIND WHISTLES PAST.

Total eclipses are rare, and don't last long—usually less than 7 minutes. In 1973, passengers on the supersonic airliner *Concorde* flew along the Moon's shadow and watched the eclipse for 74 minutes!

Fruit and vegetables harvested during a full Moon are said to have more flavor and goodness than those harvested during the Moon's other phases.

Almost all geographical features on Venus are named after females, with just a few exceptions.

SO YOU WANNA GO TO...
MERCURY

HOW BIG?

If Earth measured one inch across,
Mercury would be about the size of a pea.

ACT YOUR AGE!

Mercury's years last less than three Earth months, so if
you're ten on Earth now, you'll be over 40 on Mercury!

WHAT'S THE VIEW?

Sun, sun, sun, which appears
2½ times as large in Mercury's skies
as in Earth's and six times brighter. So is
it blue skies all year round and the perfect
holiday spot? Not really! The sky's black, and day
temperatures soar to 800°F—hot enough to melt
lead, let alone a sombrero. On the up side, it'll
never rain, as the Sun burnt off any clouds
long ago. However, temperatures drop
at night to −300°F.

DID YOU KNOW?

If you lived on Mercury you would weigh
less because Mercury has weaker gravity.
If you weighed 70 pounds on Earth, your
Mercury weight would be about 27 pounds.

VENUS...
A VISITOR'S GUIDE

HOW BIG?

If Earth measured one inch across, Venus would be just under an inch.

ACT YOUR AGE!

One year on Venus is 225 Earth days. So, if you're ten on Earth now, you'll have 16 candles on your birthday cake on Venus.

DID YOU KNOW?

The air is deadly, and temperatures are so extreme that no space probe that's landed on Venus has survived for more than a few hours.

WHAT'S THE VIEW?

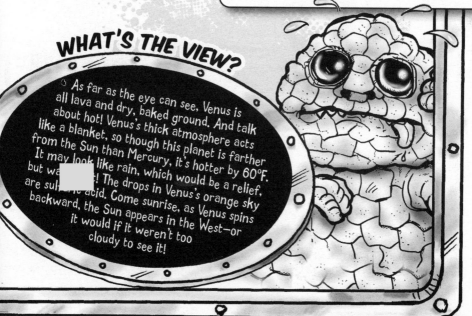

As far as the eye can see, Venus is all lava and dry, baked ground. And talk about hot! Venus's thick atmosphere acts like a blanket, so though this planet is farther from the Sun than Mercury, it's hotter by 60°F. It may look like rain, which would be a relief, but wait! The drops in Venus's orange sky are sulfuric acid. Come sunrise, as Venus spins backward, the Sun appears in the West—or it would if it weren't too cloudy to see it!

Santa sighting

Who says you can't have fun in space? In December 1965,
astronauts Walter M. Schirra Jr. and Thomas P. Stafford were
preparing to re-enter Earth's atmosphere in the

GEMINI 6 SPACECRAFT

when they told Mission Control they had just seen
Santa Claus. Schirra then played "Jingle Bells" on a
harmonica he had smuggled on board in his spacesuit,
accompanied by Stafford playing smuggled sleigh bells.

Europa, one of Jupiter's moons,
is the smoothest place we
know, with no hills or valleys.

Spaceship-shape

In July 2007, a California company called Moller advertised
the first flying saucer for sale. Don't get your bags packed for
Mars just yet though! The "saucer" is really a small hovercraft.
Its eight powerful engines allow the craft to fly 10 feet above
the ground at a speed of 50 mph. Sadly, it's probably not
going to get you anywhere close to little green men!

SHOPPING FOR SHUTTLES

In 1995, scientists discovered that hungry woodpeckers had pecked over 200 holes in the foam insulation on the space shuttle *Discovery*'s fuel tank! So, a NASA employee stopped by a Wal-Mart store in Florida to buy six plastic owls that were used to scare away the troublesome birds.

ASTRONAUTS

Space politics

U.S. astronaut David Wolf voted from space! He used email to cast his vote for the mayor of Houston, Texas, from the Russian space station *Mir*.

The fastest humans were the astronauts on the Apollo 10 mission, who reached 24,790 mph on their way back to Earth from orbiting the Moon in 1969.

Far-out fashion

To venture into space, spacesuits have to be warmed, cooled, pressurized, and supplied with fresh air. It's no wonder a spacesuit takes over six hours to put on, and costs well over a million dollars.

Smashing time

Several Russian cosmonauts struggled to re-adapt to life on Earth. Months after their flight, they would let go of a cup in mid-air and be surprised when it crashed to the floor!

A Buzz word

Buzz Aldrin was the second man on the Moon. Guess what his mom's maiden name was? Moon!

WOW!

Double trouble

Neil A. Armstrong, a 38-year-old man from Symmes Township, Ohio, receives dozens of letters and phone calls every year intended for famous astronaut Neil A. Armstrong, who lives just 11 miles away.

AMAZING!

Black hole in one?

In 2006, a golf ball hit by cosmonaut Mikhail Tyurin entered Earth's orbit. It may still be traveling around Earth now! Or, it might have fallen toward Earth and burned up when entering the atmosphere. It was hit off the International Space Station from a special tee attached to a platform, and could have covered a distance of a billion miles. Now *that's* a long shot!

NO WAY!

Weight loss

A spacesuit worn by the *Apollo* astronauts weighed only 30 pounds on the Moon, which was just as well, because it weighed in at a mighty 180 pounds on Earth! On the Moon, without Earth's gravity pulling on it, the suit became lighter.

The longest spaceflight so far has been made by the Russian cosmonaut Valeriy Polyakov, who stayed on space station Mir for 437 days.

YOU MAY KISS THE BRIDE— LATER

When Ekaterina Dmitriev married her bridegroom, Yuri Malenchenko, in Texas in 2003, he was

240 MILES

above Earth! Yuri was a Russian cosmonaut and Commander of the International Space Station at the time. In Texas, weddings are allowed where one person is absent. However, so that she wasn't lonely, Ekaterina stood next to a cardboard cut-out of her man during the satellite-linked wedding ceremony.

Litter bugs

Millions of pieces of space junk weighing more than

6,000 TONS

are in orbit around Earth. Space junk can be anything
from hatches blown off space modules, or paint
fragments from the space shuttle, to satellites that
no longer work. And they're all hurtling around us at
roughly 17,500 mph! The oldest debris up there is the
U.S. satellite *Vanguard*, which was launched in 1958
and is still orbiting Earth.

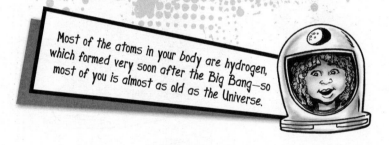

Most of the atoms in your body are hydrogen,
which formed very soon after the Big Bang—so
most of you is almost as old as the Universe.

Try harder!

When astronauts landed on the Moon, they loved
bouncing over the surface with slow, high jumps. They could
do that because the Moon's gravity is 16.6 percent that of
Earth's. So simple is it to appear super-athletic there that
the men's world long jump record, which is just over 29 feet
on Earth, would be 176 feet on the Moon. On Jupiter, where
gravity is 2½ times that on Earth, the jump would
be an unimpressive 11 feet.

Extreme diet

It's never going to happen, but if you *could* survive the heat in the center of Earth, you would find that you

WEIGHED NOTHING

and could float around, because Earth's gravity would pull you equally in all directions.

Saturn is so light it would float in your bath. (If you had a bath bigger than the planet, that is.)

A piece of the Moon

NASA created a giant moon pie in 2009 to celebrate the 40th anniversary of the first Moon landing. The special pie—consisting of marshmallow squeezed around two giant crackers and dipped in chocolate—measured 40 inches in diameter, stood 6 inches high, and weighed 55 pounds.

RIPLEY's PLAY TIME

1 Radio reports of an invasion of Earth by aliens on October 30, 1938, caused a big panic in America.

2 On hearing the story, many worried people believed that alien forces were actually invading our planet.

3 Phone lines were jammed by people spreading the news and calling the police and hospitals for advice.

4 The report was actually a play adapted by the actor Orson Welles from H.G. Wells' novel *The War of the Worlds*.

THROWING DOWN THE GAUNTLET

In 1965, the U.S. astronaut Edward White lost a glove while on the first American spacewalk from *Gemini 4*. It remained in orbit for a month, reaching speeds of

17,400 MPH!

An object traveling at that speed can cause a lot of damage to spacecraft, so the glove became the most dangerous garment in history. It joined all the other objects left in space—among them a spatula, a camera, and 480 million tiny copper needles launched as an experiment by the U.S. Airforce in 1963.

Light fantastic

The highest speed in the Universe
is the speed of light, which travels at

186,282 MILES A SECOND!

Even at this speed, it would take over four years
to reach Earth's second nearest star (after the Sun).

Jupiter gives out
much more heat
than it gets from
the Sun.

Moon dust

Dr. Eugene Shoemaker, a U.S. geologist, had
always dreamed of being an astronaut, so when
he died he wanted his ashes put on the Moon.
And in 1999 the *Lunar Prospector* spacecraft
delivered his ashes to a crater on the Moon.

UP, UP, AND AWAY

Neurolab was a 1998 space shuttle experiment to test how living creatures survived being weightless in space. It involved 1,500 crickets, 230 swordtail fish, 130 water snails, 150 rats, and 18 pregnant mice! Other strange things taken into orbit include a lightsaber handle used as a prop for Luke Skywalker in *Star Wars*, carried by Space Shuttle *Discovery*, and the ashes of actor James Doohan who played the part of Scotty in *Star Trek* and who died in 2005.

Some of Saturn's rings are kept in place by objects like small moons called shepherd moons.

The Milky Way galaxy has about 200 billion stars—about the same number of cells that are in your brain.

SO YOU WANNA GO TO...
EARTH

WHAT'S THE VIEW?

From space, Earth looks beautiful. Five million trillion trillion living things find life here good, so if you're an alien planning a visit, we can't blame you! But it's not all great news. At any one time, there are 20 volcanoes blowing their top. Every year, millions of earthquakes crack Earth's crust and 1,000 tons of space debris thump down. And meteorites hundreds of miles wide have crash-landed here in the past.

HOW BIG?

Earth measures 7,917 miles across.

ACT YOUR AGE!

The Earth's spin is slowing down so, in the future, a day may be 25 hours long and you'd be a few days younger than you are now.

DID YOU KNOW?

About 71 percent of Earth's surface is water. Hurrah! But 97 percent of this is too salty to drink. Boo! If you collected and piled up all the salt in the sea on dry land it would form a layer 500 feet high.

THE MOON...
A VISITOR'S GUIDE

HOW BIG?

If Earth measured one inch across, the Moon would be about a quarter of an inch across.

WHAT'S THE VIEW?

Just when you think everything's gray—gray dust, gray rocks, no colorful life, no water—BANG! Along comes an American flag, all red, white, and blue and left by *Apollo* missions. It doesn't move of course, because there's no weather on the Moon. In the sky, Earth, like a jewel, lies 240,000 miles in the distance but is moving gradually farther away—each full moon is 0.1 inch farther from Earth than the last.

HOW FAR?

The Moon is about 240,000 miles from Earth. If you were traveling by car at 70 mph it would take 143 days to get there!

DID YOU KNOW?

The Moon might have played a role in evolution on Earth! Wow! How? Well, the Moon's gravity controls Earth's tides and the regular rise and fall of sea levels means that life is exposed to both water and air in just a few hours. This may have sparked the spread of water creatures onto land.

WHEN YOU'VE GOTTA GO...

Going to the toilet takes 10 minutes longer in space than on Earth. And what a fuss! Astronauts have to strap themselves on to the toilet seat, using leg-restraints and thigh-bars, and connect with their

PERSONAL URINAL FUNNEL!

Then, like a vacuum cleaner, the toilet sucks air—yes, even smelly air—and waste into the pan.

Every year, 40,000 tons of cosmic dust falls to Earth—that's equivalent to the combined weight of around 250 blue whales!

Beep beep!

It's getting busy up there. Nowadays, there are about 6,000 satellites in the sky, so it's not surprising that occasionally they

into each other. In February 2009, an old Russian satellite collided with a working U.S. satellite and created at least 600 more pieces of space junk.

CANINE COSMONAUT

The first space-traveler was a dog called Laika, who was sent into space in 1957. She was a stray found wandering the streets of Moscow, when she was captured and prepared for the special space mission. In November 1957, Laika was launched in her spacecraft, *Sputnik 2*, which was no bigger than an everyday washing machine. Sadly, Laika died just a few hours after takeoff, but her space flight helped to make future space missions possible.

The Grand Moon Hotel

PARKING AROUND THE BACK

Many of Jupiter's moons orbit in the opposite direction to the way that Jupiter spins.

ZOOM TO THE MOON

Imagine the day when travel brochures advertise vacations on the Moon! Maybe it'll be slotted into the "M" listings, between Madagascar and Moscow! It's not such a fanciful notion. Dutch architect Hans-Jurgen Rombaut has designed the

FIRST MOON HOTEL!

It is supposed to be finished by 2050, and will have two tall, thin towers, thick walls, and an insulating layer of water to keep out cosmic rays and regulate the temperature indoors.

It takes moonlight 1.25 seconds to reach Earth. A full Moon is nine times brighter than a half Moon.

GALAXIES

Group hug

The Universe is a cozy place. Stars and gases are gathered together by gravity into groups called galaxies. Our own galaxy is the Milky Way and it's made of about 200 billion stars, so there's no need for anyone to feel lonely.

WOW!

Folks next door

The nearest large galaxy to the Milky Way is the Andromeda Galaxy. It is so far away that light from it takes 2.5 million years to reach us. The Milky Way is actually on a collision course with the Andromeda Galaxy, but the two won't meet until after our Sun has died!

It takes about 225 million years for our Sun to revolve once around the center of our galaxy. Wheeeeee . . .

Number crunching

There are an estimated 125 billion galaxies in the Universe, with a typical galaxy containing 50 billion to 100 billion stars. Whoa!

AMAZING!

INCREDIBLE!

E.T.A. not good

It would take the SR-71 Blackbird, the world's fastest jet, 30 billion years to get from one end of the Milky Way to the other. How depressing would those details be on the flight information board at an airport!

Long ago, most galaxies were blue, because of all the young stars being born in them.

FANTASTIC!

Camping in

If you think sleeping under the stars sounds great but gets spoiled by stony ground and chilly temperatures, there's a way of doing it in comfort. A company called StarMurals transforms bedroom ceilings with detailed galaxies of twinkling stars. A secret paint formula keeps the stars invisible by day, only for them to come out at night—just like the real thing.

AWESOME!

BLUE WITH COLD

Pack an extra sweater when you go to Uranus. There, it's always colder than the coldest winter on Earth— at round about

That's because it's so far from the Sun, has clouds made of methane ice crystals, and winds that rage at 90 mph to 360 mph! The planet is blue in color, so as well as actually being chilly, it *looks* really chilly, too.

10...9...8...oops!

Frank Sharman, from England, decided to launch his homemade model rocket into space. He built the 23-foot-long *Yellow Peril* from cardboard and molded polyester, and powered it with 14 small motors. The first attempt was scrapped after the rocket snapped in two on the launch pad. The second crashed on takeoff, setting fire to scrubland, and the third takeoff was aborted on the launch pad after a gentle summer breeze nearly blew Frank's rocket over!

SLEEPING ON YOUR FEET

When it's bedtime, astronauts climb into sleeping bags, which are fixed to the wall, and hook their arms into restraints to stop them from floating around in their sleep. They can sleep vertically or horizontally. It really doesn't matter in

ZERO GRAVITY.

On the International Space Station, if it's okay with the commander, an astronaut can sleep anywhere on board.

SPEEDY TORTOISE

On September 14, 1968, Russian tortoises were launched into space in the *Zond 5* spaceship and flew around the Moon with only mealworms and wine flies for company. They were the first animals in deep space, returning safely to Earth, after being recovered at sea on September 21.

Volcanoes on Jupiter's moon, Io, can spew out hot material at speeds of half a mile per second. That's 20 times faster than the average volcano on Earth. It's the most volcanic place in the Solar System.

Time starts now

The most powerful space telescopes can see so far away that they can observe the faint lights of galaxies on the very edge of the Universe. The light from these galaxies started traveling less than

ONE BILLION YEARS

after the beginning of the Universe. So, not only are we looking at galaxies as they looked when they were first formed, but we can almost see the start of the Universe.

Aim . . . fire!

On July 4, 2005, the spaceship *Deep Impact* flung a missile at Tempel 1, a four-mile-wide comet! Traveling at

23,000 MPH

the 820-pound missile blasted a massive hole in the comet's surface to help scientists find out what Tempel 1 was made of. And now we know one thing at least: The exterior of a comet is not hard, as previously thought, but soft and fine like talcum powder! Who'd have guessed?

MAN FROM OUTER SPACE

Anna Takhtarova and her granddaughter, Rita, were weeding potatoes near the village of Smelovka (now in Russia) in 1961 when a man in a spacesuit walked across the field. They wondered if he'd come from outer space, and he had! He was astronaut Yuri Gagarin, from the former USSR, who was the first astronaut in space and the first to orbit the Earth. He had ejected from his spacecraft, which crashed into a field, and had parachuted safely down to Earth.

NASA scientists say that the soil on Mars would be good enough to grow asparagus and turnips, but, sadly, is not fertile enough for strawberries!

SO YOU WANNA GO TO....
MARS

HOW BIG?

If Earth measured one inch across, Mars would be just over half an inch across.

ACT YOUR AGE!

One Mars year is 687 Earth days long, so you'd have to wait twice as long for your birthday to come around as on Earth. That's tragic! So, if you're ten on Earth now, you'd be just over five years old on Mars.

DID YOU KNOW?

Call it a positive or a negative, but you'd weigh less on Mars. Multiply your actual weight by 0.38 to find out what you'd weigh there. Seasons are similar to those on Earth, only longer, and temperatures are massively more extreme—summers can reach a warm 70°F, whereas winters can plummet to -220°F!

WHAT'S THE VIEW?

Take note, because scientists think Mars is the next destination for human explorers! Anyone who visits Mars might think they're wearing rose-tinted glasses because this planet's sky is pink, and the ground is red iron. Mars has clouds, frost, and, boy, does it have dust storms. Rain, though, is really unlikely. The last rainy day was more than a million years ago.

Russian cosmonaut Yuri Usachov had the ultimate pizza delivery. Instead of delivering it by moped...

...Pizza Hut arranged for the pizza to be sent by rocket to the International Space Station, 220 miles above Earth.

So, naturally, the delivery service took a little longer than the usual 30 minutes!

The pizza was topped with salami because pepperoni does not last as long and would have gone moldy. Yuk!

IF YOU NEED TO GO...

On spacewalks, astronauts wear big diapers as they sometimes need to be outside the International Space Station for hours. They're not called diapers, of course, because that doesn't sound cool enough for an astronaut. Instead, they're called MAGs, which stands for

MAXIMUM ABSORPTION GARMENTS!

Alan Shepard was the first American in space and just before takeoff he wanted to use the bathroom. "Too late," said ground control, telling him to pee in his spacesuit, even though he wasn't wearing a MAG. Still want to be an astronaut?!

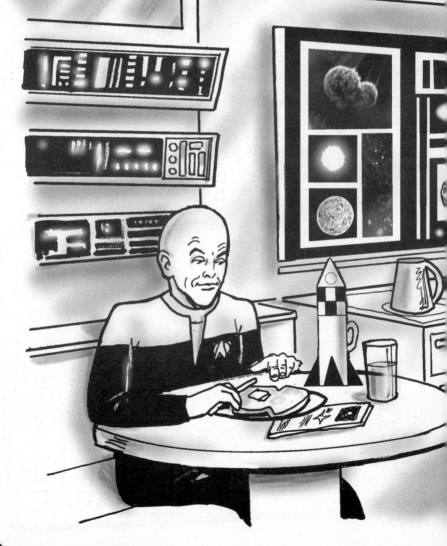

Tony Alleyne, from England, spent eight years turning his apartment into an exact replica of the spaceship U.S.S. *Enterprise* from the TV series *Star Trek: The Next Generation*. He has designed his home as a command console with flashing lights and sound effects. It has blacked-out windows to create the feeling of flying through darkest space and there's even an infinity mirror above the toilet! And of course the doorbell plays the voice of actor Patrick Stewart in his role as Captain Jean-Luc Picard!

Who'd have thought that one of the important turning points for would-be astronauts was having their

BUTT MADE INTO A MOLD?

That's because, in the early days of NASA, for reasons of comfort and safety, astronauts on manned space missions sat on couches individually molded to fit their body shape. Inside a rocket or a space station where there's

LITTLE SCOPE FOR PRIVACY

perhaps there was something comforting, too, about having your own special spot.

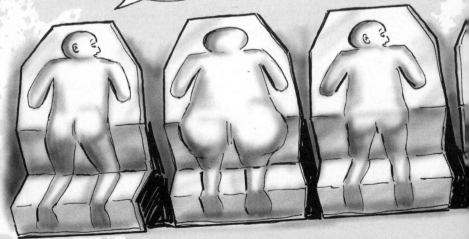

SEARCHING THE WEB

Two spiders called Arabella and Anita were kept on the Skylab space station to study the effect of

WEIGHTLESSNESS

on their ability to spin webs. It obviously took its toll, as the spiders spun uneven webs that weren't as strong as the ones they spun before takeoff.

Lights out!

Did you know that Christopher Columbus might never have been able to announce the discovery of America had it not been for an eclipse of the Moon? In the 15th century, he was held up by hostile natives in Jamaica on his way back from the New World. Knowing an eclipse was due, he said he'd make

"THE MOON LOSE HER LIGHT."

When it happened as predicted, the natives were amazed and caused no more trouble, and Chris eventually sailed back to Europe to announce his discoveries.

Did you know the planet Uranus spins on its side? This is because it had a crash with an unknown object billions of years ago.

Real story

A toy figure of *Toy Story* star Buzz Lightyear stayed in space longer than any other astronaut when it spent 15 months in orbit—beating the human record by 30 days. Toy Buzz, whose catchphrase is "To infinity and beyond!" was filmed floating weightless during his mission. He traveled on the space shuttle *Discovery* to the International Space Station in 2008 and came home to a Disney parade, where he was accompanied by Buzz Aldrin, the second man to set foot on the Moon.

SPACE TOURIST

How about a vacation in space? In 2001, U.S. businessman Dennis Tito became the world's

FIRST SPACE TOURIST.

He blasted off from Kazakhstan in a Russian Soyuz rocket for his trip to the International Space Station. He paid $20 million for his eight days in orbit.

TAKE ME TO YOUR LEADER

Every year, the town of Roswell, New Mexico, stages an Alien Pet Costume Contest. Owners dress up their animals in wacky costumes to make them look like aliens from outer space. Small dogs wearing goggles and alien headgear arrive in baby carriages that have been converted to resemble spaceships. It's not only dogs that take part. Past entrants have included pet turtles dressed in tinfoil spacesuits and ferrets with antennae on their heads. The owners often dress up and join in the fun, too!

A manned rocket reaches the Moon in less time than it used to take a coach and horses to travel the length of England!

No refuse refused

Jim Bernath from Canada collects debris from old satellites and crashed comets. His collection includes

OLD LOAVES OF BREAD

from the Russian space station *Mir* and pieces of satellites belonging to countries including Canada, Hungary, Italy, and Spain.

Half of all space-travelers get space-sick because of the weightless conditions.

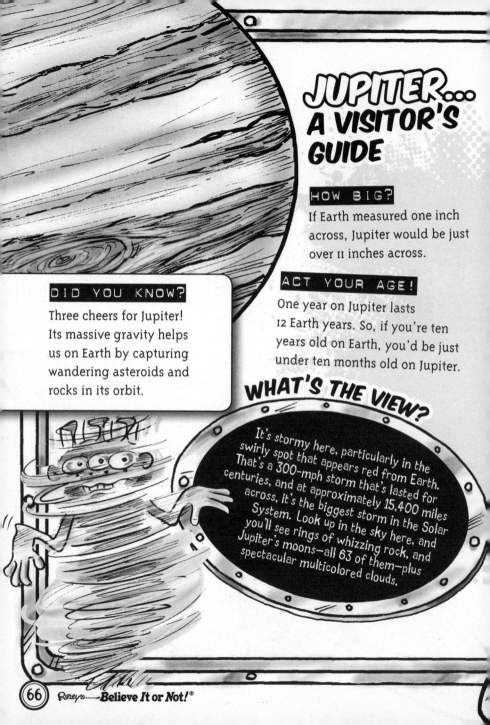

JUPITER... A VISITOR'S GUIDE

HOW BIG?

If Earth measured one inch across, Jupiter would be just over 11 inches across.

ACT YOUR AGE!

One year on Jupiter lasts 12 Earth years. So, if you're ten years old on Earth, you'd be just under ten months old on Jupiter.

DID YOU KNOW?

Three cheers for Jupiter! Its massive gravity helps us on Earth by capturing wandering asteroids and rocks in its orbit.

WHAT'S THE VIEW?

It's stormy here, particularly in the swirly spot that appears red from Earth. That's a 300-mph storm that's lasted for centuries, and at approximately 15,400 miles across, it's the biggest storm in the Solar System. Look up in the sky here, and you'll see rings of whizzing rock, and Jupiter's moons—all 63 of them—plus spectacular multicolored clouds.

SO YOU WANNA GO TO.... SATURN

Saturn's a gas planet, so, take care! Landing a spacecraft there would be like dropping in on a cloud! And while we're mentioning clouds, on Saturn they obstruct any view there might be—and they're blowing at 1,000 mph on the planet's equator. Overhead are Saturn's rings, the planet's most spectacular feature. They're huge—over 160 million miles in diameter—but super slim, the average just 50 feet thick.

HOW BIG?

If Earth measured one inch across, Saturn would be 9 inches across.

ACT YOUR AGE!

One Saturn year is equivalent to 29.6 Earth years. So, if you're ten years old on Earth, you'd be 4.5 months old on Saturn.

DID YOU KNOW?

The farthest away of the planets visible to the human eye, Saturn's rings are one of the most beautiful sights in the Universe.

STARS

Two's company
About half the stars in the Universe exist in pairs. They are called binary stars, and both stars in the pair orbit around the same point. But there are systems that have three, four, or even more stars that orbit together around the same point.

Going on a bit
The star with the longest name is Shurnarkabtishashutu, which is Arabic for "under the southern horn of the bull."

What kept you?
An exploding star (called a supernova) was seen by Chinese astronomers in AD 1054. Actually, it exploded in about 4000 BC, but the light took 5,000 years to get here.

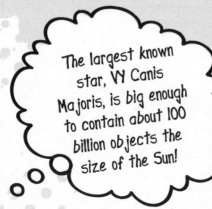

The largest known star, VY Canis Majoris, is big enough to contain about 100 billion objects the size of the Sun!

Brilliant logic
The light from most stars you can see has taken decades to get to Earth—which means you are seeing them as they were before you were born.

Long players

Stars usually last for billions of years—but the more massive stars are, the brighter they burn and the shorter period they live.

Our star, the Sun, is 860,000 miles across, but the biggest stars can be as much as 2 billion miles across.

Tripping the light fantastic

On September 28, 2006, streetlights across Iceland were switched off to give people a better view of the stars—while an astronomer speaking on the country's national radio station explained what people were seeing.

Heavy thought

Types of stars called neutron stars are so dense that a fragment the size of a sugar cube would weigh as much as all the people on Earth put together.

Star-spangled colors

Have a good look at the stars and you'll see they range in color from red to white to blue. Red is the coolest color, and is the color of stars with the least energy. Stars like our Sun are yellowish white, while the hottest stars are blue.

INTERGALACTIC WEDDING

When Rebecca D'Madeiros and Bill Duda got married in Portland, Oregon, they and all 70 guests dressed as characters from the *Star Wars* movies! The bride and groom dressed as Mon Mothma and Admiral Ackbar, the wedding was presided over by Yoda, and the ring bearer was Princess Leia. After the ceremony the newlyweds were led from the house by a line of Imperial Stormtroopers. The wedding pictures were out of this world!

Every square inch of the Sun's surface burns with the brightness of over 1.5 million candles!

Seeing stars

Our nearest star, after the Sun, is about

ONE MILLION

times farther from Earth than the nearest planet.

OUT FOR THE COUNT

We're told to count sheep when we can't get to sleep, but there are times when we've added up a whole flock and there's still no sign of shut-eye. That's when we should start counting stars, because there is an endless supply of them. Even if you counted one star every second, morning, noon, and night, it would still take you about

3,000 YEARS

to count the stars in just our own Milky Way galaxy.

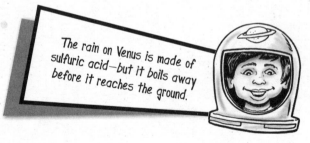

The rain on Venus is made of sulfuric acid—but it boils away before it reaches the ground.

Secret of youth

Time slows down where gravity is strong. This means that people who live on mountains, where gravity is not quite as strong, age a tiny bit faster than those at sea level.

  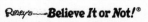

LIFE OUT THERE

Measuring the length of a football field, the International Space Station (ISS) is a step toward humans living in space. It orbits 217 miles above Earth's surface and, who knows, you might live on something similar one day.

DOWN THE PAN
When urine is released into the cold vacuum of space, it freezes into crystals, which float off in a pretty shower. What a sight!

NOT ANOTHER ONE!
The ISS orbits Earth every 92 minutes. This makes for 16 sunrises and sunsets every day, which means dawn is just after bedtime.

DRESS CODE
Koichi Wakata, a Japanese astronaut on the ISS, wore the same underpants for a whole month—and none of his 12 colleagues complained. Luckily, he wore a special pair designed to kill off nasty smells.

OOPS!
In 2008, a U.S. astronaut lost her grip on a $100,000 tool bag and it floated into space!

COSMIC CLEANING
In the weightless conditions of the ISS, water and soapsuds stick to the skin. The little water that *is* used is pulled into a drain by a fan.

HAVE FUN
Astronauts race the length of the space station for fun, but only one at a time, as the openings between modules are too small for two!

ZERO-GRAVITY GRUB
Astronauts in space mustn't eat bread, in case the crumbs float into eyes or damage equipment.

Between 1900 and 1912, one of the events in
the Olympic Games was the standing high jump.
If it had been held on the Moon, it might have
been a whole different story. The Moon has

JUST A SIXTH OF THE EARTH'S

gravity, so if the average person stood there, they
could jump 13 feet straight up—like jumping on top
of a double-decker bus!

HOW MUCH?

Here's a word of warning. If you find a meteorite, look after it carefully. For many years, the standard price for meteoritic material was just $1 per pound, but now many meteorites are worth as much as gold! Pity the poor unsuspecting finders who have already used precious fallen meteorites for such hum-drum items as blacksmith anvils and dog bowls, and for propping up cars.

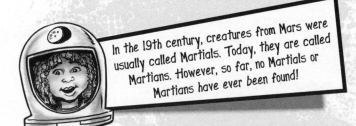

In the 19th century, creatures from Mars were usually called Martials. Today, they are called Martians. However, so far, no Martials or Martians have ever been found!

DOTTY?

Canadian Stephen Michalak, from Winnipeg, claimed
to have witnessed a UFO landing at Falcon Lake,
Manitoba, Canada, in 1967. At first he thought the
hissing noise above him was geese flying overhead,
but when he looked up he saw two red, glowing objects
that smelled of sulfur. As he got closer to the craft, he
was apparently burned, leaving him with a series of
strange dots in a grid pattern on his abdomen.

STRIKING MODEL

Ken Applegate from St. Petersburg, Florida, spent 12 years making a small-scale replica of the *Challenger* space shuttle from over half a million matchsticks. More than 12 feet long and weighing about

100 POUNDS

the matchstick model was finished in 2008 and even has moving features such as opening cargo bay doors and retractable wheels. For obvious reasons, Ken didn't add rocket fuel!

ON THE ROCKS

ASTEROIDS, COMETS, AND METEORITES

An **asteroid** is a rubbly piece of rock that whizzes around the Sun like the rest of us. Asteroids can range in size from 100 yards to 600 miles across.

Comets are like giant, dirty snowballs. They're usually pretty happy orbiting far out at the edge of the Solar System, about four trillion miles from Earth, but sometimes they go mad and swoop in toward the Sun. When this happens, they often grow two beautiful streaming tails as they warm up—a blue one made of gas, and a white one made of dust.

A **meteorite** is something from outer space that has survived coming through Earth's atmosphere and crashed into our planet.

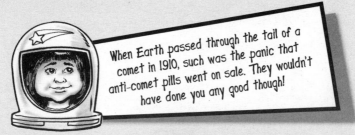

When Earth passed through the tail of a comet in 1910, such was the panic that anti-comet pills went on sale. They wouldn't have done you any good though!

AWESOME!

AMAZING!

Keep looking!

About 500 meteorites crash to Earth each year, but only about five of these are found and reported to scientists. So you'll be fairly famous if you find one and hand it in.

That's gotta hurt

A massively enormous asteroid, the size of a city, crashed into Mexico's Yucatán Peninsula 65 million years ago.

In 2000, scientists found an asteroid shaped like a dog bone. Maybe the star constellation called the Great Dog would find it tasty.

Roof justice

In 1954, in Sylacauga, Alabama, a 9-pound meteorite crashed through a roof, demolished a radio, and hit the homeowner, leaving her with bad bruising. So unlucky!

BANG!

Banana bling

A banana-shaped asteroid called 433 Eros contains precious metals worth at least $20,000 billion, including more gold than has ever been mined by humans on Earth. It orbits the Sun, mainly between Earth and Mars, and on January 31, 2012, it's expected to pass within around 16 million miles of Earth—that's about 70 times the distance to the Moon.

WOW!

HEARING YOU LOUD AND CLEAR. OVER

Thanks to special equipment, Andy Sinatra, from Brooklyn, said he was in contact with aliens. During a 1962 demonstration, he revealed that he'd been told that if the peoples of the world didn't unite within 90 days "terrible destructive forces" would be released and an invisible army of Martians would topple the U.N. building. Uh-oh!

ONE SMALL STEP FOR MAN...

The footprints left behind on the Moon by Apollo astronauts,

NEIL ARMSTRONG AND EDWIN "BUZZ" ALDRIN

more than 40 years ago are still there—just as perfect as if they were made yesterday, because there is no wind or rain to ever wipe them away. In fact, they will probably last forever.

SO YOU WANNA GO TO... URANUS

DID YOU KNOW?

Ice planets like Uranus are so dim that this one was only discovered by accident in 1781. "Hey, who are you calling dim!" Sorry, Uranus.

HOW BIG?

If Earth measured one inch across, Uranus would be 4 inches across.

ACT YOUR AGE!

A year on Uranus is equivalent to 84 years on Earth. So, if you're ten on Earth, you'd be just over 6 weeks old on Uranus! That means it would take you 84 years to reach your first birthday!

WHAT'S THE VIEW?

This planet is all ice, ice baby, so vistors should bring thermals. Uranus tilts at 98 degrees on its axis, which means it has the longest seasons in the Solar System—so if you land in winter it's going to last for the equivalent of 21 Earth years! And while we're on the subject of things lasting a while, on some parts of Uranus a flashlight might be the order of the day, as night times can be more than 40 years long.

NEPTUNE... A VISITOR'S GUIDE

HOW BIG?

If Earth measured one inch across, Neptune would be almost 4 inches across.

ACT YOUR AGE!

A year on Neptune is 165 Earth years. So, if you're ten on Earth, you'd be just over 22 days old on Neptune!

WHAT'S THE VIEW?

Here there is ice as far as the eye can see. Neptune is so far from the Sun—2,795,084,800 miles to be exact—that the Sun appears as a tiny star in Neptune's sky. You'll notice your hair blowing around a bit here, so don't get too precious about your appearance. The fastest winds in the Solar System are on Neptune, racing about at 1,200 mph.

DID YOU KNOW?

Neptune was only tracked down as a result of its effect on the way Uranus moved: It wasn't discovered until 1846.

PRESSING ON TO... PLUTO

STRIPPED OF ITS BADGE

Pluto used to be called a planet, but is now officially a humble dwarf planet. It usually orbits the Sun outside Neptune and is even colder!

ADVERTISING SPACE

Sold to the highest bidder! When Dale Gardner, an astronaut on the Space Shuttle *Discovery*, held up a "For Sale" sign in November 1984 during a space walk, he was joking that two old satellites were up for offer. In reality, advertising is becoming more space age. A well-known pizza company paid for their 30-foot-long logo to be stuck on an unmanned rocket and there has been at least one proposal for a giant billboard to be placed in low orbit—so that it could be seen from Earth!

RIPLEY's
MAY THE FORCE BE WITH YOU

Astronauts have said how hard it is to cope with the force of four times gravity (G-force) a few seconds after takeoff in an *Apollo* rocket. Think, then, of Colonel John Stapp who, in 1954, experienced a whopping 40 G when he traveled from 0 to more than 600 mph and back again in just a few seconds in a rocket-powered sled.

John hit a maximum speed of 632 mph in his rocket sled.

Then, 1.4 seconds later, he hurtled into a water barrier and stopped.

The massive G-force of this impact made John's eyeballs shoot forward.

The result was temporary blindness and two black eyes.

AMAZING MAZE

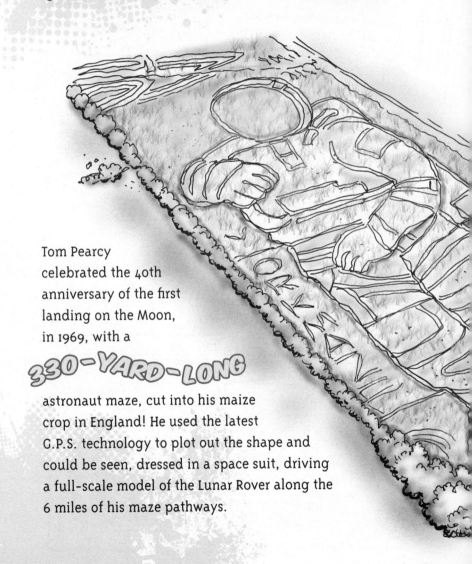

Tom Pearcy celebrated the 40th anniversary of the first landing on the Moon, in 1969, with a

330-YARD-LONG

astronaut maze, cut into his maize crop in England! He used the latest G.P.S. technology to plot out the shape and could be seen, dressed in a space suit, driving a full-scale model of the Lunar Rover along the 6 miles of his maze pathways.

Out of the blue

Where does the phrase "once in a blue moon" come from? A blue moon is the second of two full moons in one month, and occurs about once every 2¾ years—but, sorry to say, it doesn't actually change color.

Astronauts can't cry properly in space, because there's no gravity to make tears fall. Maybe space is an ideal place to peel onions!

FROM MARS TO WISCONSIN

Bob Tohak has believed in UFOs since he was a kid. So eager is he to make contact with aliens that he has erected a 42-foot-high

landing port on his property in Poland, Wisconsin. "I'm just hoping that something will show up," he says.

In 1911, a meteorite from Mars killed an Egyptian dog!

GONE ROVING

In 1997, the first ever "thinking" robot to be sent into space finally arrived on Mars. The *Pathfinder Sojourner Rover* was equipped with

LASER "EYES"

and could find its own way across the rocky surface of the planet without bumping into anything serious. During its travels, it sent over 17,000 photos back to scientists on Earth.

There is no up and no down in space, and no left or right.

HIGH-FLIERS

Surgeons operating under zero gravity? It's an image that brings to mind floating implements, and even the odd body part flying away! Not quite, but in September 2006, surgeons from Bordeaux University operated in a plane that was free-falling to create weightless conditions. They certainly battled to keep their feet on the ground. The reason for the experiment was to have a trial run for surgery on astronauts in space.

WHO ARE YOU?

Did you know that you can buy a device that seeks out aliens? The Yutan Alien Detector claims to identify changes in the atmosphere that might be signs of an alien presence. It will beep and tell you whether the person you chat with at the bus stop every morning is an alien or not, and maybe also whether you are one yourself!

If you wanted to see all of Australia, Europe, and America in less than half a day, try sitting on the Moon. It barely moves, but the Earth spins around beneath it at a much faster pace—what a mind-blowing sight!

The Olympus Mons volcano on Mars rises 16 miles into the Martian sky. Its base is so big that it would cover nearly the whole of Arizona.

You could fit as many as 60 Earths into Neptune—as long as they weren't spherical, as spheres would leave a lot of gaps around the edges!

In 1960, astronomer Frank Drake, working in West Virginia, sent radio messages to two nearby stars in the hope that intelligent aliens might reply.

Spinning at more than 1,000 times a second, some neutron stars rotate ten times faster than a compact disk.

In addition to causing tides at sea, the Moon's gravity moves the Earth's crust up and down by up to 12 inches.

It is possible that before our Universe existed there was another one, and another one before that, and another before that... .